Crochet Animal Friends

Techniques & Patterns

Consulting by Heidi Beazley

Written by Beth Taylor

Photo styling by Ewelina Rusek and Amy Stark

Photography by Christopher Hiltz
Additional photography from Getty and Shutterstock.com

Crochet symbols and abbreviations from Craft Yarn Council's www.YarnStandards.com

Louis Weber, CEO
Publications International, Ltd.
8140 Lehigh Avenue
Morton Grove, IL 60053

ISBN: 978-1-63938-495-2

Manufactured in China.

8 7 6 5 4 3 2 1

Let's get social!
@Publications_International
@PublicationsInternational
www.pilbooks.com

Table of Contents

What You'll Need

Crochet Hooks

Crochet hooks are commonly made from aluminum, plastic, wood, or bamboo. They are available in a wide range of sizes and are used with an assortment of yarns. Most patterns and yarn labels recommend a hook size. Select a crochet hook that feels comfortable to you and works well with your project and yarn.

Common Hook Sizes

U.S.	B-1	C-2	D-3	E-4	F-5	G-6	7	H-8	I-9	J-10	K-10.5	L-11	M-13	N-15	P	Q	S
mm	2.25	2.75	3.25	3.5	3.75	4	4.5	5	5.5	6	6.5	8	9	10	15	16	19

Needles

Tapestry or yarn needles have a blunt tip and an eye large enough to accommodate thick yarns. These special needles can be used to weave in yarn tails or sew crocheted pieces together.

Stitch Markers

Stitch markers are designed to mark a particular stitch, such as at the beginning of a round. They must have openings so that they can be easily removed. Purchase stitch markers, or improvise with pins, earrings, or safety pins.

Pins

Use long, rustproof pins for blocking and pinning crocheted pieces together. Select pins with large, colorful heads that won't get lost in your crochet work.

Safety Eyes and Noses

Safety eyes and noses come in various sizes and colors. They are inserted from the front (right) side like a screw, then a washer is attached on the back (wrong) side to secure them in place.

Polyfill Stuffing

Use this polyester fiber filling to stuff your crochet animals. Purchase bags at craft stores or online.

All About Yarn

Yarn for Beginners

Before starting any new crochet project, you must select your yarn. For beginners learning the basic stitches, select a simple cotton yarn that is light colored, smooth, and sturdy. It's harder to see your stitches with dark colored yarn. Avoid fuzzy and loosely woven yarns that fray easily.

Yarn Fibers

Natural fibers

Cotton, linen, and hemp yarns are made from plant fibers. They are lightweight, breathable, and machine washable. Mercerized cotton has undergone a chemical process that results in stronger, shinier yarn.

Yarns made from animal fibers include wool, silk, cashmere, mohair, alpaca, and angora. These animal fibers are much warmer than plant fibers. Both types of natural fibers offer a bit of stretch.

Synthetic fibers

Yarns made from synthetic fibers include nylon, rayon, acrylic, and polyester. Synthetic yarns are usually less expensive than natural fibers, but are less breathable and pill more easily.

Novelty and specialty yarns

Novelty and specialty yarns can be tricky to work with, but create a distinctive look. They include bouclé, ladder, eyelash, and chenille. While great for trims and accessories, novelty yarn is not best for beginners.

Selecting Your Yarn

Each package of store-bought yarn has a label listing the yarn's length, fiber content, and weight. Yarn weight refers to the thickness of a yarn. It ranges from the thinnest embroidery thread to the bulkiest yarn. Yarn labels also recommend hook size—just look for the crochet hook symbol to find the U.S. and metric (mm) hook size.

Yarn Weight Guidelines

Yarn types: Fingering, lace, and 10-count crochet thread
Recommended hook sizes (metric): 1.5–2.25 mm
Recommended hook sizes (U.S.): Steel 6 to B-1
Crochet gauge range: 32–42 double crochet stitches to 4 inches

Yarn types: Sock, fingering, and baby
Recommended hook sizes (metric): 2.25–3.5 mm
Recommended hook sizes (U.S.): B-1 to E-4
Crochet gauge range: 21–32 single crochet stitches to 4 inches

Yarn types: Sport and baby
Recommended hook sizes (metric): 3.5–4.5 mm
Recommended hook sizes (U.S.): E-4 to 7
Crochet gauge range: 16–20 single crochet stitches to 4 inches

Yarn types: Double knitting and light worsted
Recommended hook sizes (metric): 4.5–5.5 mm
Recommended hook sizes (U.S.): 7 to I-9
Crochet gauge range: 12–17 single crochet stitches to 4 inches

Yarn types: Afghan, aran, and worsted
Recommended hook sizes (metric): 5.5–6.5 mm
Recommended hook sizes (U.S.): I-9 to K-10.5
Crochet gauge range: 11–14 single crochet stitches to 4 inches

Yarn types: Chunky, craft, and rug
Recommended hook sizes (metric): 6.5–9 mm
Recommended hook sizes (U.S.): K-10.5 to M-13
Crochet gauge range: 8–11 single crochet stitches to 4 inches

Yarn types: Bulky and roving
Recommended hook sizes (metric): 9–15 mm
Recommended hook sizes (U.S.): M-13 to Q
Crochet gauge range: 7–9 single crochet stitches to 4 inches

Yarn types: Jumbo and roving
Recommended hook sizes (metric): 15 mm and larger
Recommended hook sizes (U.S.): Q and larger
Crochet gauge range: 6 single crochet stitches and fewer to 4 in.

Source: Craft Yarn Council's www.YarnStandards.com

Holding the Hook

Pencil Hold

or

Knife Hold

Tip: The instructions and photographs in this book are intended for right-handed crocheters. If you are a lefty, try holding up a mirror to the edge of a photograph to see the left-handed version.

Holding the Yarn

1

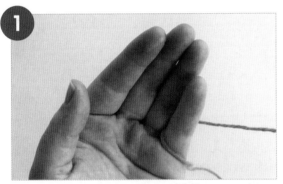

With your palm facing up, weave the working yarn (the yarn coming from the ball) between your pinky and ring fingers. Wrap the yarn clockwise around your pinky.

2

Take the yarn across your ring and middle fingers. Then wrap the yarn under and around your index finger.

3

Hold the yarn under the slip knot with your left thumb and middle finger.

Tip: There are many ways to hold your yarn. Experiment with different methods until you find what is most comfortable for you.

Making a Slip Knot

The first step in any crochet project is a slip knot.
The slip knot is what attaches the yarn to your hook.

1 Wrap the yarn around your index and middle fingers on your yarn hand to create an X.

2 From the top, insert your hook under the first loop to grab the second loop.

3 Draw the second loop you just grabbed under and up through the first loop.

4 Slide your fingers out. Pull your hook up while gently pulling both ends of the yarn down.

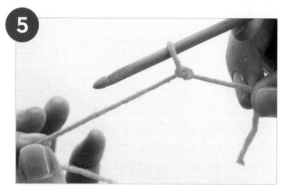

5 Pull the ends of the yarn to tighten the slip knot close to your hook.

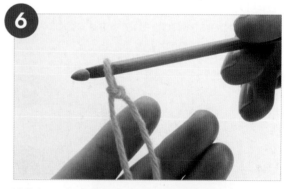

6 With a finished slip knot around your hook, you are ready to start crocheting.

Chain Stitch (ch)

Crochet often begins with a series of chain stitches used to make up the first row. This is called the foundation chain and is the basic start to most crochet projects.

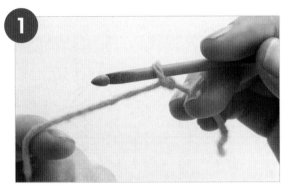

1 Start with a slip knot on your hook. Hold the yarn tail for tension.

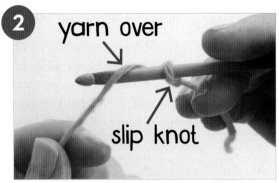

2 yarn over slip knot

Bring the working yarn (the yarn coming from the ball) over your hook from back to front. This is called yarn over (yo).

3 Draw this section of yarn back through the slip knot. You will have 1 new loop on your hook when your first chain stitch is complete.

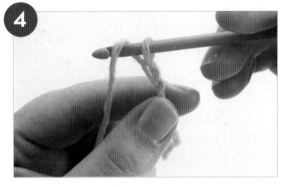

4 Yarn over again.

5 Draw this section of yarn through the loop on your hook. You will have 1 new loop on your hook each time you complete a chain stitch.

6 Repeat steps 4–5 until your foundation chain has the required number of chain stitches.

Counting Chains

Crochet patterns usually begin by telling you the number of chains needed for the foundation chain.

Identifying the Front and Back

The front of the foundation chain looks like a braid with a series of Vs. The back side of the foundation chain has a vertical ridge of bumps running down the middle from your hook to the end of the chain. Count chains from the front side.

Front   **Back**

Counting

Begin counting from the top of the foundation chain. (You can also count from the bottom up.) Do not count the loop on your hook or the slip knot on the bottom. Count only completed, V-shaped chain stitches. This example has 13 completed chain stitches.

- -

Tip: When creating a long foundation chain, it is helpful to use stitch markers every 10 or 20 stitches to make counting easier.

- -

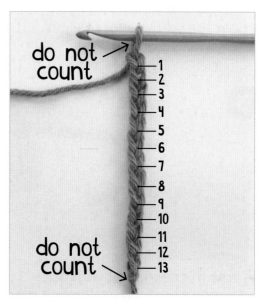

do not count

1
2
3
4
5
6
7
8
9
10
11
12
13

do not count

Turning Chains (tch)

Stitch	Number of Turning Chains
Slip stitch	0
Single crochet	1
Half double crochet	2
Double crochet	3
Treble crochet	4

Each crochet stitch requires a specific number of turning chains at the beginning or end of a row. The number of extra stitches needed for the turning chain is added to the number needed for the foundation chain.

Tension

Tension keeps your stitches neat and consistent. Make sure the chains in your foundation chain are even and loose enough to allow your hook back into those chains for the next row.

Too loose

Too tight

Just right

Slip Stitch (sl st)

The slip stitch is one of the most basic crochet stitches and is often used for joining.

1

Start with a foundation chain on your hook. Insert your hook from front to back into the second chain from your hook. There are 2 loops on your hook.

2

Yarn over, bringing the working yarn over your hook from back to front.

3

Draw the yarn through both loops on your hook. You will have 1 new loop on your hook when your first slip stitch is complete.

Single Crochet (sc)

How to single crochet:

To begin a row of single crochet, first stitch a foundation chain to the desired length. Add 1 extra chain stitch for the turning chain.

insert your hook into this stitch →

Insert your hook from front to back into the second chain stitch from your hook. There will now be 2 loops on your hook.

Yarn over. Draw this yarn through the first loop on your hook. There will be 2 loops on your hook.

3

Yarn over again and draw this yarn through both loops on your hook. You will have 1 loop remaining on your hook when your first single crochet is complete.

4

insert your hook into this stitch

Insert your hook into the next chain stitch. Repeat steps 2–3 to complete another single crochet stitch.

5

Repeat step 4, working a single crochet stitch into each chain. At the end of the row, make 1 chain stitch for the turning chain.

6

insert your hook into this stitch

Turn your work so that the opposite side faces you. Insert your hook into the first single crochet stitch of the previous row and repeat steps 2–3. (Skip the turning chain.)

7

Insert your hook into the next stitch and repeat steps 2–3, working a single crochet stitch into each single crochet of the previous row.

8

Repeat step 7 to continue the pattern. At the end of this and all subsequent rows, chain 1 for the turning chain and turn your work.

Half Double Crochet (hdc)

How to half double crochet:

To begin a row of half double crochet, first stitch a foundation chain to the desired length. Add 2 extra chain stitches for the turning chain.

insert hook into this stitch

Yarn over. With this yarn over, insert your hook into the third chain stitch from your hook. There will be 3 loops on your hook.

Yarn over again. Draw the yarn through the first loop only. There will still be 3 loops on your hook.

3

Yarn over and draw the yarn through all 3 loops on your hook.

4

You will have 1 loop on your hook when your first half double crochet is complete.

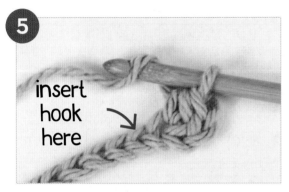

5

insert hook here

Yarn over. With this yarn over, insert your hook into the next chain stitch. There will be 3 loops on your hook. Repeat steps 2–4 to complete another half double crochet stitch.

6

Repeat step 5, working a half double crochet stitch into each chain stitch. At the end of the row, chain 2 for the turning chain.

7

insert hook into this stitch

Turn your work so that the opposite side faces you. Yarn over and insert your hook into the second stitch. (The turning chain counts as the first half double crochet stitch in this row.) Repeat steps 2–4 to complete the half double crochet stitch.

8

Repeat step 5 to continue making half double crochet stitches into each stitch of the previous row. At the end of this and all subsequent rows, chain 2 for the turning chain and turn.

Double Crochet (dc)

How to double crochet:

To begin a row of double crochet, first stitch a foundation chain to the desired length. Add 3 extra chain stitches for the turning chain.

1

insert hook into this stitch

Yarn over. With this yarn over, insert your hook into the fourth chain stitch from your hook. There will be 3 loops on your hook.

2

Yarn over. Draw the yarn through the first loop on your hook. There will be 3 loops on your hook.

3

Yarn over. Draw the yarn through the first 2 loops on your hook only. There will now be 2 loops on your hook.

4

Yarn over again. Draw the yarn through the remaining 2 loops on your hook. You will have 1 loop on your hook when your first double crochet is complete.

5

insert hook here

Yarn over. Insert your hook into the next chain stitch. Repeat steps 2–4 to complete another double crochet stitch.

6

Repeat step 5, working a double crochet stitch into each chain stitch. At the end of the row, chain 3 for the turning chain. Turn your work so that the opposite side faces you.

7

insert your hook into this stitch

Yarn over and insert your hook into the second stitch. (The turning chain counts as the first double crochet stitch in this row.) Repeat steps 2–4 to complete the double crochet stitch.

8

Repeat step 5 to continue making double crochet stitches into each stitch of the previous row. At the end of this and all subsequent rows, chain 3 for the turning chain and turn.

Treble Crochet (tr)

How to treble crochet:

To begin a row of treble crochet, first stitch a foundation chain to the desired length. Add 4 extra chain stitches for the turning chain.

insert your hook into this stitch ➝

Yarn over twice. Insert your hook into the fifth chain stitch from your hook. There will be 4 loops on your hook.

Yarn over once. Draw the yarn through the first loop on your hook. There will be 4 loops on your hook.

3

Yarn over once. Draw the yarn through the first 2 loops on your hook. There will be 3 loops on your hook.

4

Yarn over once. Draw the yarn through the first 2 loops on your hook again. There will be 2 loops on your hook.

5

Yarn over once. Draw the yarn through the remaining 2 loops on your hook. You will have 1 loop on your hook when your first treble crochet is complete.

6

insert your hook into this stitch

Yarn over twice and insert your hook into the next chain stitch. Repeat steps 2–5 to complete another treble crochet stitch.

7

insert your hook into this stitch

Repeat step 6, working a treble crochet stitch into each chain. At the end of the row, chain 4 for the turning chain. Turn your work so that the opposite side faces you. Yarn over twice and insert your hook into the second stitch. Repeat steps 2–5 to complete the treble crochet stitch.

8

Repeat step 6 to continue making treble crochet stitches into each stitch of the previous row. At the end of this and all subsequent rows, chain 4 for the turning chain and turn.

Decreasing Stitches (dec)

To decrease within a row, combine multiple stitches together.

Single Crochet 2 Together (sc2tog) _____

Insert your hook into the next stitch as you would to start a single crochet.

Yarn over and draw the yarn through the stitch. There are now 2 loops on your hook.

Insert your hook into the next stitch. Yarn over and draw the yarn through the stitch. There are 3 loops on your hook.

Yarn over and draw the yarn through all 3 loops on your hook. You will have 1 loop on your hook when your first single crochet decrease (sc2tog) is complete.

Double Crochet 2 Together (dc2tog) _____

Yarn over and insert your hook into the next stitch. Yarn over and draw the yarn through the stitch. Yarn over and draw the yarn through the first 2 loops. You will have 2 loops on your hook.

Yarn over and insert your hook into the next stitch. Yarn over and draw the yarn through the stitch. Yarn over and draw the yarn through the first 2 loops. You will have 3 loops on your hook.

3

Yarn over and draw the yarn through all 3 loops on your hook. You will have 1 loop on your hook when your first double crochet decrease (dc2tog) is complete.

Increasing Stitches (inc)

To increase within a row, work multiple stitches into the same stitch.

Single Crochet Increase (sc inc)

1

Insert your hook back into the same stitch you did your last single crochet in. Work another single crochet into that same stitch.

2

You will have 1 loop on your hook when your first single crochet increase is complete.

Double Crochet Increase (dc inc)

1

Insert your hook back into the same stitch in the previous row. Work another double crochet into that same stitch.

2

You will have 1 loop on your hook when your first double crochet increase is complete.

Front & Back Loops (FL & BL)

Working into the front or back loop only will create a unique texture and line. These examples use half double crochet, but you can use these techniques with other stitches.

Tip: When your crochet work is in front of you, the front loop is the loop closer to you, while the back loop is farther from you.

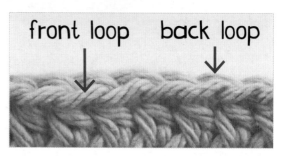

front loop   back loop

Front Loops

1

To work a half double crochet stitch into the front loop only (flo), yarn over and insert your hook into only the front loop closer to you. Complete the stitch as usual.

2

Continue working half double crochet stitches into only the front loops of the stitches in the previous row until you reach the end of the row. This creates a line.

Back Loops

1

To work a half double crochet stitch into the back loop only (blo), yarn over and insert your hook into only the back loop farther from you. Complete the stitch as usual.

2

Continue working half double crochet stitches into only the back loops of the stitches in the previous row until you reach the end of the row. This creates another line.

Working in Rounds

To begin working in rounds, you have to first start with a center ring. There are 2 different methods for starting a round, with a chain stitch ring or a magic circle.

Chain Stitch Ring

The chain stitch ring is made up of chain stitches that are joined together to form a ring. This method leaves a small opening in the center of your round.

- -

Tip: Patterns will tell you how many chains to start with and what stitches to use. This example uses single crochet.

- -

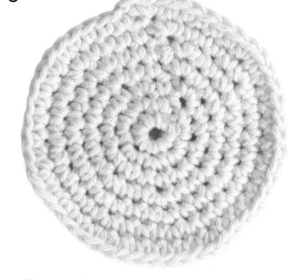

1 Chain 5 for a foundation chain. Insert your hook back into the first chain you made.

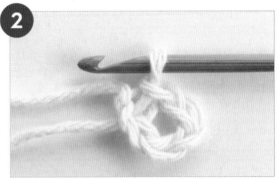

2 Work a slip stitch into that chain to form a ring.

3 Insert your hook into the center of the ring. Work a single crochet stitch into the ring.

4 Continue working single crochet stitches into the ring until you have made the required number of stitches. (For this example, 6 single crochet stitches.)

Work a slip stitch into the first single crochet you made to close up the ring.

You are now ready to start a round. (See page 26.)

Magic Circle

The magic circle forms a ring with your yarn to which your first round of stitches are attached. The ends are pulled to leave no opening in the center. That's the magic!

- -

Tip: A chain stitch ring can replace a magic circle in a pattern.

- -

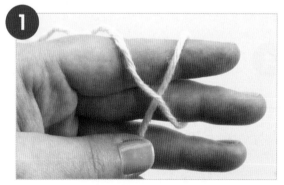

Loop the yarn around your fingers as shown to form an X.

Take your hook under the bottom strand of the X. Use your hook to draw the other strand under the bottom strand. It will form a loose loop on your hook.

3

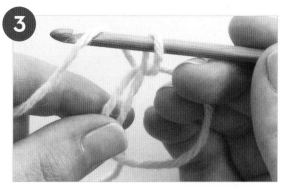

Remove the circle of yarn from your fingers. Yarn over. Draw the yarn through the loop on your hook. (This does not count as your first single crochet stitch.)

4

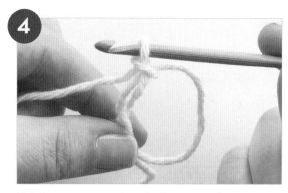

With your magic circle complete, you should now have a circle with the tail and the working yarn on the left side.

5

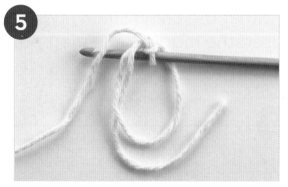

Insert your hook into the center of the circle. You are going to work a single crochet into that space. Yarn over and draw the yarn through the circle and tail. You will have 2 loops on your hook.

6

Yarn over again and draw the yarn through the remaining 2 loops on your hook. You will have 1 loop on your hook when your first single crochet stitch into the circle is complete.

7

Continue working the required number of single crochet stitches into the circle, making sure you are always working around the circle and the tail. If you run out of tail, pull it slightly. This closes the circle a little, but allows you to have a longer tail to work around.

8

When you have worked 6 single crochet stitches into the circle, pull the tail tightly to close the circle.

Insert your hook into the first single crochet stitch you made and make a slip stitch to close the circle.

With your slip stitch complete, you are now ready to start a round.

Starting a Round

To start a round, first begin by using either the chain stitch ring or magic circle method. This example used the magic circle method.

Round 1:

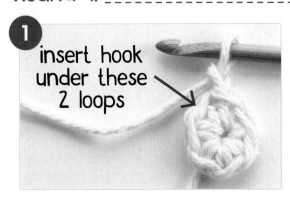

insert hook under these 2 loops

Chain 1. Insert your hook under the top 2 loops of the first stitch and work a single crochet into that stitch.

Work 2 single crochets into each of the remaining stitches. (You will have 12 stitches.) Insert your hook back into the first stitch and make a slip stitch to close the round.

Rounds 2-6:

Each round increases by 6 stitches. The increases are evenly spaced in order to keep the circular shape. Close each round with a slip stitch back into the first stitch and then chain 1.

Round 2: Single crochet an increase in every other stitch for a total of 18 stitches.
Round 3: Single crochet an increase in every third stitch for a total of 24 stitches.
Round 4: Single crochet an increase in every fourth stitch for a total of 30 stitches.
Round 5: Single crochet an increase in every fifth stitch for a total of 36 stitches.
Round 6: Single crochet an increase in every sixth stitch for a total of 42 stitches.

For additional rounds, continue to evenly increase your rounds by 6 until reaching your desired circumference.

Joining in New Yarn

At the End of a Row --

1

To join in new yarn at the end of a row, work the last stitch with the old yarn until the final yarn over of the stitch. Yarn over with the new yarn.

2

Draw the new yarn through both loops on your hook. There is 1 loop on your hook. Continue stitching with the new yarn as usual.

In the Middle of a Row --

1

To join in new yarn in the middle of a row, work the last stitch with the old yarn until the final yarn over of the stitch. Yarn over with the new yarn.

2

Draw the new yarn through both loops on your hook. There is 1 loop on your hook. Continue stitching with the new yarn as usual until you reach the end of the row.

Tip: Rather than leaving the tail of the old yarn in the middle of the row, you can work over the old yarn until you reach the end of the row. You can then weave in all yarn tails at the edges later.

Fastening Off

After completing your last stitch, cut the excess yarn, leaving several inches to weave the tail in later. Yarn over and draw the yarn tail through the loop on your hook.

Pull the yarn tail to tighten.

Weaving in the Tail

Thread one of your yarn tails into a blunt-tipped needle. Insert the needle into the first stitch and draw the yarn through.

Continue weaving the needle under and over the stitches around the edge.

- -

Cut the yarn close to the final stitch when you're done weaving in the tail.

- -

Abbreviations & Symbols

Crochet patterns often use abbreviations and symbols as shorthand to represent frequently used stitches and techniques. Use the guide below as you start to follow patterns using shorthand.

Abbreviations

alt	alternate
approx	approximately
beg	begin/beginning
bet	between
BL or blo	back loop or back loop only
bo	bobble
BP	back post
BPdc	back post double crochet
BPhdc	back post half double crochet
BPsc	back post single crochet
BPtr	back post treble crochet
CC	contrasting color
ch	chain(s)
ch-sp	chain space(s)
CL	cluster
cm	centimeter(s)
cont	continue
dc	double crochet(s)
dec	decrease(s)/decreasing
dtr	double treble crochet(s)
FL or flo	front loop or front loop only
FP	front post
FPdc	front post double crochet
FPhdc	front post half double crochet
FPsc	front post single crochet
FPtr	front post treble crochet
hdc	half double crochet(s)
hk	hook
inc	increase(s)/increasing
lp(s)	loop(s)
MC	main color
mm	millimeter(s)

p	picot
pc	popcorn
pat(s)	pattern(s)
pm	place marker
prev	previous
rem	remain/remaining
rep	repeat(s)
rnd(s)	round(s)
RS	right side
sc	single crochet(s)
sl st	slip stitch
sk	skip
sp(s)	space(s)
st(s)	stitch(es)
tch	turning chain(s)
tog	together
tr	treble crochet(s)
WS	wrong side
yd(s)	yard(s)
yo	yarn over
" or in	inch(es)
[ ]	work instructions within brackets as many times as directed
( )	work instructions within parentheses as many times as directed
*	repeat the instructions following the single asterisk as directed
**	repeat the instructions between asterisks as many times as directed or repeat from a given set of instructions

Symbols

⬯	chain
•	slip stitch
X or †	single crochet
	half double crochet
	double crochet
	treble crochet
	sc2tog
	sc3tog
	dc2tog
	dc3tog
	3-dc cluster
	3-hdc cluster/ puff st/bobble
	5-dc popcorn
	5-dc shell
	ch-3 picot
	front post dc
	back post dc
⌢	worked in back loop only**
⌣	worked in front loop only**

**Symbol appears at base of stitch being worked

Bunny

Other: Pins, polyfill stuffing, small pom-pom maker, 14 mm safety eyes, 13 mm safety nose, stitch marker, tapestry needle

Skill Level

EASY

Materials

 Velvet yarn, 246 yards

Hook: 5 mm/U.S. H-8

Stitches Used

Chain stitch (ch)
Magic circle
Single crochet (sc)
Single crochet 2 together (sc2tog)
Single crochet increase (sc inc)
Slip stitch (sl st)

Instructions

Use a stitch marker to mark the first stitch of each round. Move the stitch marker up as you work.

Head

Make a magic circle.

Round 1: 6 sc in magic circle.

Round 2: Sc inc in each st around.

Round 3: *Sc, sc inc; rep from * around.

Round 4: *2 sc, sc inc; rep from * around.

Round 5: *3 sc, sc inc; rep from * around.

Round 6: *4 sc, sc inc; rep from * around.

Round 7: *5 sc, sc inc; rep from * around.

Round 8: *6 sc, sc inc; rep from * around.

Round 9: *7 sc, sc inc; rep from * around.

Rounds 10–20: Sc in each st around.

Tip: Sc increase: Work a single crochet into next stitch, inserting hook under top 2 loops of stitch. Work another single crochet into that same stitch to complete the sc inc.

Adding the Eyes and Nose

Step 1: From the front (right) side of the bunny's head, push one of the safety eyes through a space between stitches in rounds 15 and 16 from front to back.

Step 2: Attach the plastic washer to the safety eye from the back (wrong) side, inside the bunny's head.

Step 3: From the front (right) side, insert other safety eye about 8 stitches over from the first eye between rounds 15 and 16. Attach plastic washer on back side.

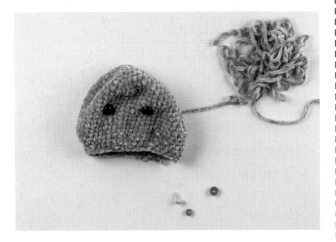

Step 4: From the front (right) side of the bunny's head, insert the safety nose from front to back 2 rounds down and centered between the eyes.

Step 5: Attach the plastic washer on the back (wrong) side, inside the bunny's head.

Tip: Safety eyes and noses are inserted from the front (right) side like a screw, then a washer is attached on the back (wrong) side to secure in place.

After adding safety eyes and nose, begin stuffing head with polyfill as you continue each round.

Round 21: *7 sc, sc2tog; repeat from * around.

Round 22: *6 sc, sc2tog; repeat from * around.

Round 23: *5 sc, sc2tog; repeat from * around.

Round 24: *4 sc, sc2tog; repeat from * around.

Round 25: *3 sc, sc2tog; repeat from * around.

Round 26: *2 sc, sc2tog; repeat from * around.

Round 27: *Sc, sc2tog; rep from * around.

Round 28: Sc2tog around.

Finish stuffing head with polyfill.

Fasten off, leaving a long tail with which to close the remaining hole and sew the head onto the body later.

Body

The body will begin at the bottom of the legs and work up to the top. Stuff with polyfill as you go.

Make a magic circle.

Tip: How to sc2tog: [Insert hook in next stitch, yo, draw yarn through stitch] 2 times, yo, draw yarn through all 3 loops on hook to complete the sc2tog.

Round 1: 6 sc in magic circle.

Round 2: Sc inc in each st around.

Round 3: *Sc, sc inc; rep from * around.

Rounds 4–28: Sc in each st around.

Fasten off. Repeat above for second leg, but do not fasten off after round 28.

Ch 3.

Round 29: Sc into the next stitch of the first leg, and in each stitch around and over the 3 chains to the second leg until you reach your stitch marker.

Rounds 30–45: Sc in each st around.

Round 46: *4 sc, sc2tog; rep from * around.

Round 47: *3 sc, sc2tog; rep from * around.

Round 48: *2 sc, sc2tog; rep from * around.

Round 49: *Sc, sc2tog; rep from * around.

Round 50: Sc in each st around.

Fasten off.

Arms (make 2)

Stuff arms with polyfill as you go.

Make a magic circle.

Round 1: 6 sc in magic circle.

Rounds 2–22: Sc in each st around.

Fasten off, leaving a long tail with which to sew arms onto body.

Ears (make 2)

Do not stuff ears.

Make a magic circle.

Round 1: 6 sc in magic circle.

Round 2: Sc inc in each st around.

Round 3: *Sc, sc inc; rep from * around.

Rounds 4–16: Sc in each st around.

Round 17: Sc2tog in each st around.

Fasten off, leaving a long tail with which to sew ears onto head.

Tail

With 4/medium yarn of your choice, make a small pom-pom tail. We used less than 3 yards of contrasting white yarn, but you'll have enough leftover velvet yarn to make pom-pom tail. Open up both arms of pom-pom maker. Wrap yarn around one arm desired number of times. More wraps makes a thicker pom-pom. Bring yarn across top of center wheel and then wrap around 2nd arm same number of times as first arm. Close both arms of pom-pom maker. Cut excess yarn. Place scissors into groove on one side and cut through center of one wrapped arm. Repeat for other wrapped arm. Cut a 12" length of matching yarn. Wrap yarn around pom-pom maker, along groove where you cut. Tie 2 really tight knots on one side. Wrap yarn around to other side and tie 2 really tight knots on that side. Open up arms and pull halves apart to release pom-pom. Leave 2 long ends to attach tail to body.

Assembly

Thread the long tail left from the head through a tapestry needle. Sew head securely to body all the way around. Pin arms to body in desired position. Thread long tail from arm through tapestry needle. Sew arms onto body. Pin ears to head in desired position. Thread long tail from ear through tapestry needle. Sew ears onto head. Attach pom-pom tail to back of body using 2 long ends. Weave in all yarn tails when done.

Tip: This completed bunny is about 15" tall from top of head to bottom of legs.

Tip: **Stitch markers:** Stitch markers are especially critical when crocheting amigurumi. Because you frequently do not join at the end of each round, you need to know exactly which stitch marks the beginning and/or end of each round.

Frog

Skill Level

EASY

Materials

 364-yard skein in green (you'll have yarn leftover), plus 6–8" of black scrap yarn for mouth

Hook: 4 mm/U.S. G-6
Other: Pins, polyfill stuffing, 13 mm safety eyes, stitch marker, tapestry needle

Stitches Used

Chain stitch (ch)

Magic circle

Single crochet (sc)

Single crochet 2 together (sc2tog)

Slip stitch (sl st)

Instructions

Use a stitch marker to mark the beginning of each round.

Eyes (make 2)

Make a magic circle.

Round 1: 8 sc in magic circle.

Round 2: *2 sc in next st, sc in each of next 3 sts; repeat from * around.

Round 3: 2 sc in next st, sc in next 2 sts, 2 sc in next st, sc in next 6 sts.

Fasten off after first eye. Do not fasten off after second eye.

Connecting the Eyes

Step 1: While still attached to 2nd eye, ch 4.

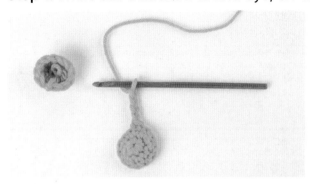

Step 2: Slip stitch in last stitch of first eye.

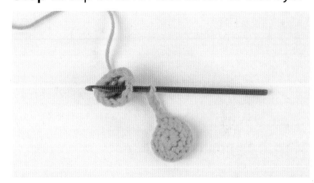

Step 3: Single crochet in each stitch around first eye until you reach ch 4.

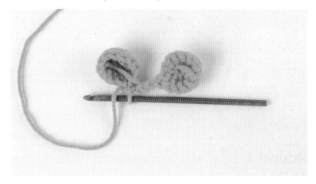

Step 4: Single crochet in the back bumps only of 4 ch stitches.

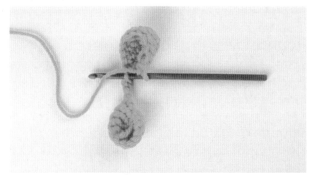

Step 5: Sc in first st of 2nd eye and in each st around until you reach middle ch 4 sts.

Step 6: Sc in each of middle ch 4 sts.

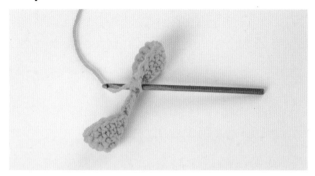

Step 7: Continue to sc in each st around.

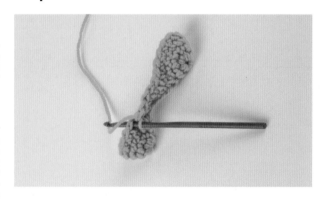

Head/Body

Round 1: Sc in each st around, making the sc sts in the top of middle ch 4 sts.

Round 2: 2 sc in each of next 3 sts, sc in next 17 sts, 2 sc in each of next 3 sts, sc in next 9 sts.

Round 3: 2 sc in next st, sc in each of next 7 sts, 2 sc in next st, sc in each of next 8 sts, 2 sc in next st, sc in each of next 8 sts, 2 sc in next st, sc in each of next 11 sts.

Rounds 4–10: Sc in each st around. Add two 13 mm safety eyes. (See pages 31–32.) Begin stuffing with polyfill as you go.

Round 11: *Sc2tog, sc in next 5 sts; rep from * around.

Round 12: *2 sc in next st, sc in each of next 5 sts; rep from * around.

Round 13: *2 sc in next st, sc in each of next 6 sts; rep from * around.

Round 14: *2 sc in next st, sc in each of next 7 sts; rep from * around.

Rounds 15–22: Sc in each st around.

Round 23: *Sc2tog, sc in each of next 7 sts; rep from * around.

Round 24: *Sc2tog, sc in each of next 6 sts; rep from * around.

Round 25: *Sc2tog, sc in each of next 5 sts; rep from * around.

Round 26: *Sc2tog, sc in each of next 4 sts; rep from * around.

Round 27: *Sc2tog, sc in each of next 3 sts; rep from * around.

Round 28: *Sc2tog, sc in each of next 2 sts; repeat from * around. Finish firmly stuffing.

Round 29: *Sc2tog, sc in next st; repeat from * around.

Round 30: Sc2tog in each st around. Fasten off and stitch bottom closed. Weave in ends.

Legs (make 2)

Do not stuff legs. Make a magic circle.

Round 1: 6 sc in magic circle.

Round 2: 2 sc in each st around.

Rounds 3–5: Sc in each st around.

Round 6: *Sc2tog, sc in next st; repeat from * around.

Rounds 7–22: Sc in each st around. Fasten off, leaving long tail for sewing.

Arms (make 2)

Do not stuff arms. Make a magic circle.

Round 1: 6 sc in magic circle.

Round 2: *2 sc in next st, sc in each of next 2 sts; rep from * around.

Rounds 3–14: Sc in each st around. Fasten off, leaving long tail for sewing.

Assembly

Pin both arms and legs into desired position. With a tapestry needle threaded with yarn tail, sew each arm and leg onto frog body. With strand of black scrap yarn, sew mouth on frog.

Whale

Materials

 less than 120 yards

Hook: 4 mm/U.S. G-6
Other: Polyfill stuffing, 8 mm safety eyes, stitch marker, tapestry needle

Stitches Used

Magic circle
Single crochet (sc)
Single crochet 2 together (sc2tog)

Instructions

Use a stitch marker to mark the beginning of each round.

Tail Fin (make 2)

Make a magic circle.

Round 1: 4 sc in magic circle.

Round 2: *2 sc in next st, sc in next st; repeat from * around.

Round 3: *2 sc in next st, sc in each of next 2 sts; repeat from * around.

Round 4: Sc in each st around.

Round 5: *2 sc in next st, sc in each of next 3 sts; repeat from * around.

Round 6: Sc in each st around.

After completing first tail fin, fasten off, leaving long tail for sewing.

After completing 2nd tail fin, do not fasten off, but keep working: Join 2nd tail fin to first tail fin with a sc in st after final st of round 6, and sc in each st around.

Do not fasten off, but continue following pattern for body.

Body

Round 1: *Sc2tog, sc in each of next 2 sts; repeat from * around.

Using the long tail from first tail fin and a tapestry needle, sew together the space remaining from where the tail fins were joined together.

Round 2: *Sc2tog, sc in each of next 3 sts; repeat from * around.

Round 3: Sc in each st around.

Round 4: *2 sc in next st, sc in next st; repeat from * around.

Round 5: 2 sc in next st, sc in each of next 4 sts, *2 sc in next st, sc in each of next 2 sts; repeat from * 2 more times, sc in each of next 4 sts.

Stuff tail fins with polyfill stuffing.

Round 6: Sc in next 5 sts, 2 sc in next st, sc in next 3 sts, 2 sc in next st, sc in next 2 sts, 2 sc in next st, sc in next 3 sts, 2 sc in next st, sc in each of next 5 sts.

Round 7: Sc in next 6 sts, 2 sc in next st, sc in next 3 sts, 2 sc in next st, sc in next 4 sts, 2 sc in next st, sc in next 3 sts, 2 sc in next st, sc in next 6 sts.

Round 8: Sc in next 6 sts, 2 sc in next st, sc in next 3 sts, 2 sc in next st, *sc in next 2 sts, 2 sc in next st; repeat from * 3 times, sc in next 3 sts, 2 sc in next st, sc in next 6 sts.

Round 9: Sc in next 11 sts, 2 sc in next st, sc in next 12 sts, 2 sc in next st, sc in next 11 sts.

Round 10: *Sc in next 12 sts, 2 sc in next st; repeat from * 2 times, sc in next 12 sts.

Round 11: Sc in next 13 sts, 2 sc in next st, sc in next 12 sts, 2 sc in next st, sc in next 13 sts.

Rounds 12–18: Sc in each st around.

Round 19: *Sc2tog, sc in next 5 sts; repeat from * around.

Round 20: *Sc2tog, sc in next 4 sts; repeat from * around.

Round 21: *Sc2tog, sc in next 3 sts; repeat from * around.

Begin to stuff whale body with polyfill stuffing.

Round 22: *Sc2tog, sc in next 2 sts; repeat from * around.

Attach two 8 mm safety eyes between rounds 18 and 19, about 12 sts apart, closer to underside of whale. (See pages 31–32 for how to attach safety eyes.)

Round 23: *Sc2tog, sc in next st; repeat from * around.

Finish stuffing whale body with polyfill.

Round 24: *Sc2tog; repeat from * around.

Fasten off, leaving tail for sewing. Sew remaining hole closed and weave in ends.

Fins (make 2)

Make a magic circle.

Round 1: 4 sc in magic circle.

Round 2: 2 sc in each st around.

Rounds 3–5: Sc in each st around.

Fold the fin flat, and sc along both sides to close. Fasten off, leaving long tail with which to sew fin onto body. Sew fins to sides of whale, starting about 3 rows behind eyes.

Tip: **How to sc2tog:** [Insert hook in next stitch, yarn over, draw yarn through stitch] 2 times, yarn over, draw yarn through all 3 loops on hook to complete the sc2tog.

Tip: The finished whale is about 6" long by 3½" high.

Skunk

Skill Level

INTERMEDIATE

Materials

364-yard skeins in black and white (you'll have plenty of yarn leftover, especially in white)

Hook: 4 mm/U.S. G-6
Other: Pins, polyfill stuffing, 13 mm safety eyes, 13 mm safety nose, stitch marker, tapestry needle

Stitches Used

Chain stitch (ch)
Magic circle
Single crochet (sc)
Single crochet 2 together (sc2tog)

Instructions

Use a stitch marker to mark the beginning of each round.

Body

With black yarn, make a magic circle. Stuff body firmly with polyfill as you go.

Round 1: 6 sc in magic circle.

Round 2: 2 sc in each st around.

Round 3: *2 sc in next st, sc in next st; rep from * around.

Round 4: *2 sc in next st, sc in each of next 2 sts; rep from * around.

Round 5: *2 sc in next st, sc in each of next 3 sts; rep from * around.

Round 6: *2 sc in next st, sc in each of next 4 sts; rep from * around.

Round 7: *2 sc in next st, sc in each of next 5 sts; rep from * around.

Round 8: *2 sc in next st, sc in each of next 6 sts; rep from * around.

Rounds 9–15: Sc in each st around.

Round 16: *Sc2tog, sc in each of next 6 sts; rep from * around.

Rounds 17–18: Sc in each st around.

Round 19: *Sc2tog, sc in each of next 5 sts; rep from * around.

Rounds 20–21: Sc in each st around.

Round 22: *Sc2tog, sc in each of next 4 sts; rep from * around.

Rounds 23–24: Sc in each st around.

Round 25: *Sc2tog, sc in each of next 3 sts; rep from * around.

Rounds 26–27: Sc in each st around.

Round 28: *Sc2tog, sc in each of next 2 sts; rep from * around.

Rounds 29–30: Sc in each st around.

Fasten off and weave in end.

Head

With black yarn, make a magic circle.

Round 1: 6 sc in magic circle.

Round 2: 2 sc in each st around.

Round 3: *2 sc in next st, sc in next st; rep from * around.

Round 4: *2 sc in next st, sc in each of next 2 sts; rep from * around.

Round 5: *2 sc in next st, sc in each of next 3 sts; rep from * around.

Round 6: *2 sc in next st, sc in each of next 4 sts; rep from * around.

Round 7: *2 sc in next st, sc in each of next 5 sts; rep from * around.

Round 8: *2 sc in next st, sc in each of next 6 sts; rep from * around.

Round 9: *2 sc in next st, sc in each of next 7 sts; rep from * around.

Rounds 10–18: Sc in each st around.

Add two 13 mm safety eyes between rounds 13 and 14, about 9 sts apart. (See pages 31–32 for attaching safety eyes.) Begin lightly stuffing head.

Round 19: *Sc2tog, sc in each of next 7 sts; rep from * around.

Round 20: *Sc2tog, sc in each of next 6 sts; rep from * around.

Round 21: *Sc2tog, sc in each of next 5 sts; rep from * around.

Round 22: *Sc2tog, sc in each of next 4 sts; rep from * around.

Round 23: *Sc2tog, sc in each of next 3 sts; rep from * around.

Round 24: *Sc2tog, sc in each of next 2 sts; rep from * around.

Round 25: *Sc2tog, sc in each st around; rep from * around.

Round 26: *Sc2tog; rep from * around.

Fasten off, leaving long tail for sewing.

Muzzle

With black yarn, make a magic circle.

Round 1: 6 sc in magic circle.

Round 2: 2 sc in each st around.

Rounds 3–4: Sc in each st around.

Round 5: *2 sc in next st, sc in next st; rep from * around.

Round 6: Sc in each st around.

Round 7: *2 sc in next st, sc in each of next 2 sts; rep from * around.

Round 8: Sc in each of next 9 sts, 2 sc in each of next 6 sts, sc in each of next 9 sts.

Add 13 mm safety nose at tip of muzzle.

Ears (make 2)

With black yarn, make a magic circle.

Round 1: 6 sc in magic circle.

Round 2: 2 sc in each st around.

Rounds 3–5: Sc in each st around.

Fasten off, leaving long tail for sewing.

Arms (make 2)

Make a magic circle. Lightly stuff bottom of arms only.

Round 1: 6 sc in magic circle.

Round 2: 2 sc in each st around.

Round 3: *2 sc in next st, sc in each of next 3 sts; rep from * around.

Rounds 4–5: Sc in each st around.

Round 6: *Sc2tog, sc in next st; rep from * around.

Rounds 7–18: Sc in each st around.

At the end of round 18, pinch arm flat and make 5 sc sts across top to close. Fasten off, leaving long tail with which to sew arm onto body later.

Legs (make 2)

With black yarn, make a magic circle. Stuff legs with polyfill as you go.

Round 1: 6 sc in magic circle.

Round 2: 2 sc in each st around.

Round 3: *2 sc in next st, sc in next st; rep from * around.

Round 4: *2 sc in next st, sc in each of next 2 sts; rep from * around.

Round 5: Sc in back loop only of each st around.

Round 6: Sc in each st around.

Round 7: Sc in next 6 sts, sc2tog 6 times, sc in next 6 sts.

Round 8: Sc in next 3 sts, sc2tog 6 times, sc in next 3 sts.

Rounds 9–21: Sc in each st around.

Fasten off, leaving long tail for sewing onto body.

Tail

Beginning with white yarn, make a magic circle. Stuff tail firmly with polyfill as you go.

Round 1: 6 sc in magic circle.

Round 2: 2 sc in each st around.

Rounds 3–4: Sc in each st around.

Round 5: *2 sc in next st, sc in next st; rep from * around.

Round 6: Sc in each st around.

Round 7: *2 sc in next st, sc in each of next 2 sts; rep from * around.

Change to black yarn.

Round 8: With black, *2 sc in next st, sc in each of next 3 sts; rep from * around.

Round 9: *2 sc in next st, sc in each of next 4 sts; rep from * around.

Rounds 10–14: Sc in each st around.

Round 15: *Sc2tog, sc in each of next 4 sts; rep from * around.

Round 16: *Sc2tog, sc in each of next 3 sts; rep from * around.

Rounds 17–18: Sc in each st around.

Round 19: *Sc2tog, sc in each of next 2 sts; rep from * around.

Rounds 20–26: Sc in each st around.

At the end of round 26, pinch tail flat and make 9 sc sts across top to close. Fasten off, leaving long tail for sewing onto body.

Stripes (make 2)

With white yarn, chain 61. Sc in 2nd ch from hook and in each ch across. Fasten off, leaving long tail for sewing.

Assembly

Using a tapestry needle and yarn tails, assemble skunk as follows. Pin each part onto body in desired position before sewing.

1. Sew ears onto either side of head.
2. Sew muzzle onto head under eyes, stuffing with polyfill as you go.
3. Sew head onto body.
4. Sew arms onto either side of body.
5. Sew legs onto bottom of body.
6. Sew tail onto back of body.
7. Add stripes following instructions on next page.

Adding the Stripes

Step 1: Pin first white stripe from muzzle to base of tail, with long yarn tail from stripe near skunk's tail.

Step 3: Continue pinning 2nd white stripe down entire back, with long yarn tail near base of skunk's tail.

Step 2: Pin 2nd white stripe down center of body starting from same spot where first white stripe started on muzzle.

Step 4: Once stripes are pinned to your liking, thread tapestry needle with long yarn tail. Insert needle into stripe and body.

Step 5: Draw needle under and over stripe and body until complete. Loop knot when done and bring needle out at another part of body. Trim yarn. Repeat for 2nd stripe.

Turtle

Skill Level

INTERMEDIATE

Materials

 MEDIUM 4 120-yard skeins in 3 colors

Hook: 5 mm/U.S. H-8
Other: Polyfill stuffing, 8 mm safety eyes, stitch marker, tapestry needle

Stitches Used

Chain stitch (ch)
Magic circle
Single crochet (sc)
Single crochet 2 together (sc2tog)
Single crochet join
Slip stitch (sl st)
Whipstitch

Instructions

Use a stitch marker to mark the beginning of each round.

Head

With tan yarn, make a magic circle.

Round 1: 6 sc in magic circle.

Round 2: 2 sc in each st around.

Round 3: Sc in each st around.

Round 4: *2 sc in next st, sc in next st; repeat from * around.

Round 5: *2 sc in next st, sc in each of next 2 sts; repeat from * around.

Rounds 6–8: Sc in each st around.

Round 9: *Sc2tog, sc in each of next 2 sts; repeat from * around.

Rounds 10–11: Sc in each st around.

Add two 8 mm safety eyes between rounds 6 and 7, approximately 6–7 sts apart. (See pages 31–32 for safety eyes.)

Round 12: *Sc2tog, sc in next st; repeat from * around.

Start stuffing with polyfill.

Rounds 13–16: Sc in each st around.

Fasten off, leaving long tail.

Finish stuffing head, flatten open end and whipstitch closed using tail. (See whip-stitch instructions on next page.) Leave tail for sewing to shell later.

Front Legs (make 2)

With same tan yarn color as head, make a magic circle.

Round 1: 6 sc in magic circle.

Round 2: 2 sc in each st around.

Round 3: *2 sc in next st, sc in next st; repeat from * around.

Rounds 4–6: Sc in each st around.

Round 7: [Sc2tog] 4 times, sc in each remaining st around.

Round 8: Sc in each st around.

Round 9: 2 sc in next st, [sc2tog] 2 times, sc in each remaining st around.

Rounds 10–12: Sc in each st around.

Fasten off, leaving long tail. Stuff lightly with polyfill. Whipstitch closed.

How to Whipstitch

Step 1: Thread tapestry needle with yarn tail. Pinch opening closed.

Step 2: Insert needle from front to back through first pair of stitches on the right.

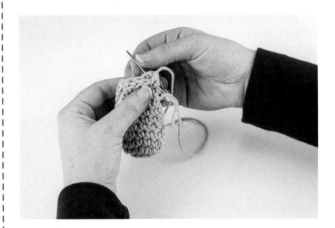

Step 3: Bring needle up over the top and insert from front to back through next pair of stitches on left.

Step 4: Repeat across seam. Leave tail for sewing to shell later.

Back Legs (make 2)

With same tan yarn color as head and front legs, make a magic circle.

Round 1: 6 sc in magic circle.

Round 2: 2 sc in each st around.

Round 3: *2 sc in next st, sc in next st; repeat from * around.

Round 4: Sc in each st around.

Round 5: [Sc2tog, sc in each of the next 7 sts] 2 times.

Round 6: [Sc2tog, sc in each of the next 6 sts] 2 times.

Rounds 7–8: Sc in each st around.

Begin adding some polyfill stuffing.

Round 9: [Sc2tog, sc in each of the next 5 sts] 2 times.

Round 10: [Sc2tog, sc in each of the next 4 sts] 2 times.

Rounds 11–12: Sc in each st around.

Fasten off, leaving long tail. Finish lightly stuffing with polyfill, flatten open ends and whipstitch together using tail. Leave tail for sewing to shell later.

Shells (make 2)

For top shell, alternate between sage green and meadow green yarn. Top shell should end with meadow green. Use meadow green for bottom shell.

Make a magic circle.

Round 1: 6 sc in magic circle.

Round 2: 2 sc in each st around.

Round 3: *2 sc in next st, sc in next st; rep from * around.

Round 4: *2 sc in next st, sc in each of next 2 sts; rep from * around.

Round 5: *2 sc in next st, sc in each of next 3 sts; rep from * around.

Round 6: *2 sc in next st, sc in each of next 4 sts; rep from * around.

Round 7: *2 sc in next st, sc in each of next 5 sts; rep from * around.

Round 8: *2 sc in next st, sc in each of next 6 sts; rep from * around.

Round 9: *2 sc in next st, sc in each of next 7 sts; rep from * around.

Round 10: *2 sc in next st, sc in each of next 8 sts; rep from * around.

Round 11: *2 sc in next st, sc in each of next 9 sts; rep from * around.

Round 12: *2 sc in next st, sc in each of next 10 sts; rep from * around.

Fasten off and weave in ends.

Assembly

With wrong side of bottom shell facing up, sew head and legs of turtle to inside of shell using tapestry needle threaded with tan yarn tail.

Step 1: Insert needle through leg (or head) and shell, weaving under and over across seam until secure.

Step 2: Weave needle through a few stitches in shell. Don't tie knot when done. Trim yarn tail.

Step 3: Once head and legs are attached, place top shell on turtle with right side facing up (wrong sides of both shells pressed together).

Step 4: Insert crochet hook through an edge stitch in both shell layers. Yarn over with new yarn. Draw yarn through.

Step 5: Yarn over again and draw yarn through to join with a slip stitch.

Step 6: Insert hook through next pair of edge stitches on both shells to the left. Complete a single crochet stitch.

Step 7: Continue making sc sts in each pair of edge sts until you reach a leg. Tuck yarn tail from join between shells. Insert hook through edge st in top shell only. Sc as usual through top shell only until end of leg.

Step 8: After leg, continue making sc sts through top and bottom shells as before. Repeat process around until before you reach starting spot. Leave small hole to stuff body with polyfill. Then complete sc edge. Fasten off and weave in ends.

Fox

Skill Level

INTERMEDIATE

Materials

364-yard skeins in orange, black, and white (you'll have plenty of yarn leftover, especially in white and black)

Hook: 4 mm/U.S. G-6
Other: Polyfill stuffing, 11 mm safety eyes, stitch marker, tapestry needle

Stitches Used

Magic circle
Single crochet (sc)
Single crochet 2 together (sc2tog)

Instructions

Use a stitch marker to mark the beginning of each round.

Body

With orange yarn, make a magic circle. Stuff firmly with polyfill as you go.

Round 1: 6 sc in magic circle.

Round 2: 2 sc in each st around.

Round 3: *2 sc in next st, sc in next st; rep from * around.

Round 4: *2 sc in next st, sc in each of next 2 sts; rep from * around.

Round 5: *2 sc in next st, sc in each of next 3 sts; rep from * around.

Round 6: *2 sc in next st, sc in each of next 4 sts; rep from * around.

Round 7: *2 sc in next st, sc in each of next 5 sts; rep from * around.

Round 8: *2 sc in next st, sc in each of next 6 sts; rep from * around.

Rounds 9–15: Sc in each st around.

Round 16: *Sc2tog, sc in each of next 6 sts; rep from * around.

Rounds 17–18: Sc in each st around.

Round 19: *Sc2tog, sc in each of next 5 sts; rep from * around.

Rounds 20–21: Sc in each st around.

Round 22: *Sc2tog, sc in each of next 4 sts; rep from * around.

Rounds 23–24: Sc in each st around.

Round 25: *Sc2tog, sc in each of next 3 sts; rep from * around.

Rounds 26–27: Sc in each st around.

Round 28: *Sc2tog, sc in each of next 2 sts; rep from * around.

Rounds 29–30: Sc in each st around.

Fasten off and weave in end.

Head

With orange yarn, make a magic circle.

Round 1: 6 sc in magic circle.

Round 2: 2 sc in each st around.

Round 3: *2 sc in next st, sc in next st; rep from * around.

Round 4: *2 sc in next st, sc in each of next 2 sts; rep from * around.

Round 5: *2 sc in next st, sc in each of next 3 sts; rep from * around.

Round 6: *2 sc in next st, sc in each of next 4 sts; rep from * around.

Round 7: *2 sc in next st, sc in each of next 5 sts; rep from * around.

Round 8: *2 sc in next st, sc in each of next 6 sts; rep from * around.

Round 9: *2 sc in next st, sc in each of next 7 sts; rep from * around.

Rounds 10–18: Sc in each st around.

Add two 11 mm safety eyes between rounds 16 and 17, about 8 sts apart. (See pages 31–32 for attaching safety eyes.) Begin lightly stuffing head.

Round 19: *Sc2tog, sc in each of next 7 sts; rep from * around.

Round 20: *Sc2tog, sc in each of next 6 sts; rep from * around.

Round 21: *Sc2tog, sc in each of next 5 sts; rep from * around.

Round 22: *Sc2tog, sc in each of next 4 sts; rep from * around.

Round 23: *Sc2tog, sc in each of next 3 sts; rep from * around.

Continue to stuff head firmly.

Round 24: *Sc2tog, sc in each of next 2 sts; rep from * around.

Round 25: *Sc2tog, sc in the next st; rep from * around.

Round 26: *Sc2tog; rep from * around.

Fasten off, leaving long tail.

Closing the Head

Step 1: Thread tapestry needle with yarn tail. Insert needle under front loop only in stitch beside where you just finished.

Step 2: Continue inserting needle under front loop only in each stitch around.

Step 3: Pull yarn tail like a drawstring to close opening.

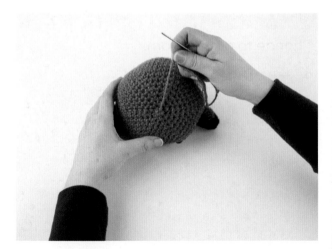

Step 4: Bring needle out elsewhere on body and trim excess yarn.

Muzzle

Beginning with white yarn, make a magic circle.

Round 1: 6 sc in magic circle.

Round 2: 2 sc in each st around.

Rounds 3–4: Sc in each st around.

Round 5: *2 sc in next st, sc in next st; rep from * around.

Round 6: Sc in each st around.

Round 7: *2 sc in next st, sc in each of next 2 sts; rep from * around.

Round 8: Sc in each st around.

Change to orange yarn.

Round 9: With orange, *2 sc in next st, sc in each of next 3 sts; rep from * around.

Fasten off, leaving long tail for sewing muzzle onto head later.

Nose

With black yarn, make a magic circle.

Round 1: 8 sc in magic circle.

Round 2: Sc in each st around.

Fasten off, leaving long tail for sewing nose onto muzzle later.

Ears (make 2)

Beginning with black yarn, make a magic circle.

Round 1: 8 sc in magic circle.

Round 2: Sc in each st around.

Round 3: *2 sc in next st, sc in next st; rep from * around.

Change to orange yarn.

Round 4: With orange, sc in each st around.

Round 5: *2 sc in next st, sc in each of next 2 sts; rep from * around.

Rounds 6–8: Sc in each st around.

Fasten off, leaving long tail for sewing ear onto head later.

Tail

Beginning with white yarn, make a magic circle. Stuff tail lightly with polyfill as you go.

Round 1: 6 sc in magic circle.

Round 2: Sc in each st around.

Round 3: 2 sc in each st around.

Round 4: *2 sc in next st, sc in next st; rep from * around.

Round 5: *2 sc in next st, sc in each of next 2 sts; rep from * around.

Round 6: *2 sc in next st, sc in each of next 3 sts; rep from * around.

Rounds 7–9: Sc in each st around.

Change to orange yarn.

Rounds 10–15: With orange, sc in each st around.

Round 16: *Sc2tog, sc in each of next 3 sts; rep from * around.

Rounds 17–18: Sc in each st around.

Round 19: *Sc2tog, sc in each of next 2 sts; rep from * around.

Rounds 20–21: Sc in each st around.

Round 22: *Sc2tog, sc in next st; rep from * around.

Rounds 23–26: Sc in each st around.

Fasten off, leaving long tail for sewing tail onto body later.

Arms (make 2)

Beginning with black yarn, make a magic circle. Lightly stuff bottom of arms only.

Round 1: 6 sc in magic circle.

Round 2: 2 sc in each st around.

Round 3: *2 sc in next st, sc in each of next 3 sts; rep from * around.

Rounds 4–5: Sc in each st around.

Round 6: *Sc2tog, sc in next st; rep from * around.

Rounds 7–11: Sc in each st around.

Change to orange yarn.

Rounds 12–18: With orange, sc in each st around.

At end of round 18, pinch arm flat and make 5 sc sts across top to close. Fasten off, leaving long tail with which to sew arm onto body later.

Tip: How to sc2tog: [Insert hook in next stitch, yo, draw yarn through stitch] 2 times, yo, draw yarn through all 3 loops on hook to complete the sc2tog.

Legs (make 2)

Beginning with black yarn, make a magic circle. Stuff legs with polyfill as you go.

Round 1: 6 sc in magic circle.

Round 2: 2 sc in each st around.

Round 3: *2 sc in next st, sc in next st; rep from * around.

Round 4: *2 sc in next st, sc in each of next 2 sts; rep from * around.

Round 5: Sc in back loop only of each st around.

Round 6: Sc in each st around.

Round 7: Sc in next 6 sts, sc2tog 6 times, sc in next 6 sts.

Round 8: Sc in next 3 sts, sc2tog 6 times, sc in next 3 sts.

Rounds 9–14: Sc in each st around.

Change to orange yarn.

Rounds 15–21: With orange, sc in each st around.

Fasten off, leaving long tail with which to sew leg onto body later.

Assembly

Using a tapestry needle and yarn tails left from various body parts, assemble the fox as follows.

1. Sew ears to either side of head.
2. Sew muzzle to head directly under eyes, stuffing with polyfill as you go.
3. Sew nose to tip of muzzle.
4. Sew head onto body.
5. Sew arms on either side of body.
6. Sew legs underneath body.
7. Sew tail to back of body. Weave in all ends.

Bear

Skill Level

EASY

Materials

380-yard skeins in light brown and cream (you'll have leftover yarn, especially in cream), plus 12" black scrap yarn

Hook: 4 mm/U.S. G-6
Other: Pins, polyfill stuffing, 10 mm safety eyes, stitch marker, tapestry needle

Stitches Used

Magic circle
Single crochet (sc)
Single crochet 2 together (sc2tog)
Single crochet join

Instructions

Use a stitch marker to mark the beginning of each round.

Head and Body

Head and body are worked as one piece, starting with the head. With light brown yarn, make a magic circle.

Round 1: 6 sc in magic circle.

Round 2: 2 sc in each st around.

Round 3: *2 sc in next st, sc in next st; rep from * around.

Round 4: *2 sc in next st, sc in each of next 2 sts; rep from * around.

Round 5: *2 sc in next st, sc in each of next 3 sts; rep from * around.

Round 6: *2 sc in next st, sc in each of next 4 sts; rep from * around.

Round 7: *2 sc in next st, sc in each of next 5 sts; rep from * around.

Round 8: *2 sc in next st, sc in each of next 6 sts; rep from * around.

Round 9: *2 sc in next st, sc in each of next 7 sts; rep from * around.

Round 10: *2 sc in next st, sc in each of next 8 sts; rep from * around.

Round 11: *2 sc in next st, sc in each of next 9 sts; rep from * around.

Rounds 12–25: Sc in each st around.

Round 26: *Sc2tog, sc in each of next 9 sts; rep from * around.

Round 27: *Sc2tog, sc in each of next 8 sts; rep from * around.

Round 28: *Sc2tog, sc in each of next 7 sts; rep from * around.

Round 29: *Sc2tog, sc in each of next 6 sts; rep from * around.

Round 30: Sc in front loop only of each st around. Add two 10 mm safety eyes between rounds 17 and 18, about 7–8 sts apart. (See pages 31–32 for safety eyes.) Begin stuffing head with polyfill.

Round 31: *2 sc in next st, sc in each of next 6 sts; rep from * around.

Round 32: Sc in each st around.

Round 33: *2 sc in next st, sc in each of next 7 sts; rep from * around.

Round 34: Sc in each st around.

Round 35: *2 sc in next st, sc in each of next 8 sts; rep from * around.

Round 36: Sc in each st around.

Round 37: *2 sc in next st, sc in each of next 9 sts; rep from * around.

Round 38: Sc in each st around.

Round 39: *2 sc in next st, sc in each of next 10 sts; rep from * around.

Rounds 40–52: Sc in each st around.

Round 53: *Sc2tog, sc in each of next 10 sts; rep from * around.

Round 54: *Sc2tog, sc in each of next 9 sts; rep from * around.

Round 55: *Sc2tog, sc in each of next 8 sts; rep from * around.

Round 56: *Sc2tog, sc in each of next 7 sts; rep from * around.

Round 57: *Sc2tog, sc in each of next 6 sts; rep from * around.

Round 58: *Sc2tog, sc in each of next 5 sts; rep from * around.

Round 59: *Sc2tog, sc in each of next 4 sts; rep from * around.

Round 60: *Sc2tog, sc in each of next 3 sts; rep from * around. Stuff body with polyfill.

Round 61: *Sc2tog, sc in each of next 2 sts; rep from * around.

Round 62: *Sc2tog, sc in next st; rep from * around.

Round 63: Sc2tog around. Fasten off, leaving long tail. With tapestry needle and tail, sew bottom closed and weave in end.

Arms (make 2)

With light brown yarn, make a magic circle.

Round 1: 6 sc in magic circle.

Round 2: 2 sc in each st around.

Round 3: *2 sc in next st, sc in next st; rep from * around.

Round 4: *2 sc in next st, sc in each of next 2 sts; rep from * around.

Round 5: *2 sc in next st, sc in each of next 3 sts; rep from * around.

Rounds 6–8: Sc in each st around.

Round 9: *Sc2tog, sc in each of next 3 sts; rep from * around.

Rounds 10–21: Sc in each st around. Stuff arm with polyfill.

Single Crochet Join

Step 1: Flatten the arm opening so that stitches line up.

Step 2: Insert your hook from front to back under the first pair of stitches on the right.

Step 3: Yarn over and draw through the loop on your hook. Yarn over and draw through both loops on your hook.

Step 4: With your first single crochet done, insert your hook under the next pair of stitches and work another single crochet.

Step 5: Continue working a single crochet into each pair of stitches across the seam.

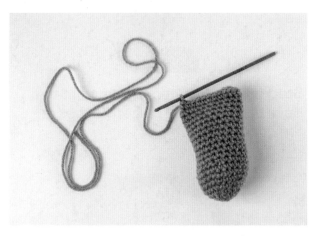

Fasten off, leaving long tail.

Legs (make 2)

Beginning with cream yarn, make a magic circle.

Round 1: 6 sc in magic circle.

Round 2: 2 sc in each st around.

Round 3: *2 sc in next st, sc in next st; rep from * around.

Round 4: *2 sc in next st, sc in next 2 sts; rep from * around.

Round 5: *2 sc in next st; sc in each of next 3 sts; rep from * around.

Round 6: *2 sc in next st; sc in each of next 4 sts; rep from * around.

Round 7: Sc in each st around.

Change to light brown yarn.

Rounds 8–9: With light brown, sc in each st around.

Round 10: *Sc2tog, sc in each of next 4 sts; rep from * around.

Round 11: *Sc2tog, sc in each of next 3 sts; rep from * around.

Rounds 12–23: Sc in each st around. Stuff leg and flatten opening so that stitches line up. Sc along opening through both sts to close leg. Fasten off, leaving long tail.

Ears (make 2)

With light brown yarn, make a magic circle.

Round 1: 6 sc in magic circle.

Round 2: 2 sc in each st around.

Round 3: *2 sc in next st, sc in next st; rep from * around.

Round 4: *2 sc in next st, sc in each of next 2 sts; rep from * around.

Round 5: *2 sc in next st, sc in each of next 3 sts; rep from * around.

Rounds 6–8: Sc in each st around. Flatten ear opening so that stitches line up. Sc along opening through both sts to close ear. Fasten off, leaving long tail.

Muzzle

With cream yarn, make a magic circle.

Round 1: 6 sc in magic circle.

Round 2: 2 sc in each st around.

Round 3: *2 sc in next st, sc in next st; rep from * around.

Round 4: *2 sc in next st, sc in each of next 2 sts; rep from * around.

Round 5: *2 sc in next st, sc in each of next 3 sts; rep from * around.

Round 6: *2 sc in next st, sc in each of next 4 sts; rep from * around. Fasten off, leaving long tail.

Making the Nose

Using the strand of black scrap yarn and a tapestry needle, embroider a nose.

Step 1: Thread a tapestry needle with strand of black scrap yarn.

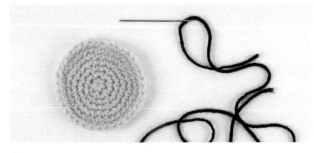

Step 2: With right (front) side of muzzle facing up, bring needle up from back to front on one side and down from front to back on opposite side.

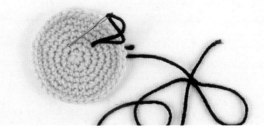

Step 3: Bring needle up from same place as before and insert down through opposite side again to create horizontal part of nose.

Step 4: To create triangle shape, make narrower lines across each subsequent row. Bring needle up from below and insert down at tip of triangle.

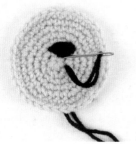

Step 5: Bring needle up from same place as before and insert down at tip of triangle again to double over part you just did. Trim yarn. You don't need to knot anything on wrong (back) side of muzzle.

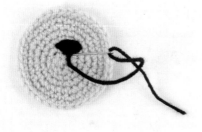

Assembly

Using a tapestry needle and yarn tails, assemble bear as follows. Pin each part onto body in desired position before sewing.

1. Sew ears onto either side of head.
2. Sew muzzle onto head under eyes, stuffing lightly with polyfill.
3. Sew on arms and legs: bring threaded needle under loop in body, then through arm or leg. Continue drawing needle through part of body, then part of limb, across seam. Loop knot when done and bring needle out of body far from limb attachment. Trim yarn.
4. Make sure all ends are woven in.

Cat

Other: Fabric glue (optional), pins, polyfill stuffing, 8 mm safety eyes, 13 mm safety nose, stitch marker, tapestry needle

Skill Level

INTERMEDIATE

Materials

120-yard skeins in gray and ecru (you'll have leftover yarn), plus two 4" scraps of black yarn

Hook: 4 mm/U.S. G-6

Stitches Used

Chain stitch (ch)

Magic circle

Single crochet (sc)

Single crochet 2 together (sc2tog)

Slip stitch (sl st)

Whipstitch

Instructions

Use a stitch marker to mark the beginning of each round. Move the stitch marker up as you work.

Head

With gray yarn, make a magic circle. Stuff head firmly with polyfill as you go.

Round 1: 6 sc in magic circle.

Round 2: 2 sc in each st around.

Round 3: *2 sc in next st, sc in next st; rep from * around.

Round 4: *2 sc in next st, sc in each of next 2 sts; rep from * around.

Round 5: *2 sc in next st, sc in each of next 3 sts; rep from *around.

Round 6: *2 sc in next st, sc in each of next 4 sts; rep from * around.

Rounds 7–11: Sc in each st around.

Add two 8 mm safety eyes between rounds 8 and 9, approximately 5–6 sts apart. (See pages 31–32 for attaching safety eyes.)

Round 12: *Sc2tog, sc in each of next 4 sts; rep from * around.

Round 13: *Sc2tog, sc in each of next 3 sts; rep from * around.

Round 14: *Sc2tog, sc in each of next 2 sts; rep from * around.

Round 15: In back loop only, *sc2tog, sc in next st; rep from * around.

Round 16: Sc2tog around.

Fasten off. Sew bottom of head closed: insert threaded tapestry needle through back loop only of each stitch around, pulling every few stitches to close like a drawstring. Leave long tail for sewing.

Muzzle

With ecru yarn, make a magic circle.

Round 1: 4 sc in magic circle.

Round 2: 2 sc in each st around.

Round 3: *2 sc in next st, sc in next st; rep from * around.

Add 13 mm safety nose at tip of muzzle.

Ears (make 2)

With gray yarn, make a magic circle.

Round 1: 3 sc in magic circle.

Round 2: 2 sc in each st around.

Round 3: *2 sc in next st, sc in next st; rep from * around.

Round 4: *2 sc in next st, sc in each of next 2 sts; rep from * around.

Round 5: *2 sc in next st, sc in each of next 3 sts; rep from * around.

Whipstitch closed: Flatten ear so sts are lined up. Insert threaded tapestry needle from front to back through first pair of sts on right. Draw yarn through, leaving tail to weave in later. Bring needle up over the top and insert from front to back through next pair of sts on left. Repeat across seam. (See page 46 for more detailed whipstitch instructions.) Fasten off, leaving long tail for sewing onto head later.

Tail

Beginning with ecru yarn, make a magic circle. Stuff tail lightly as you go.

Round 1: 5 sc in magic circle.

Round 2: Sc in each st around.

Change to gray yarn.

Rounds 3–11: With gray, sc in each st around.

Fasten off, leaving long tail for sewing.

Back Legs (make 2)

With gray yarn, make a magic circle.

Round 1: 6 sc in magic circle.

Round 2: *2 sc in next st, sc in next st; rep from * around.

Rounds 3–4: Sc in each st around.

Fasten off first leg. Do not fasten off after 2nd leg. Continue following instructions for body.

Body

Continue to crochet from the legs. Stuff as you go. Connect the legs: Ch 2, sl st into last st of first leg. Sc in each st around, including the ch 2.

Round 1: Sc in each of next 7 sts, 2 sc in next st, sc in each of next 5 sts, 2 sc in next st, sc in each of next 8 sts.

Round 2: Sc in each of next 8 sts, 2 sc in next st, sc in each of next 2 sts, 2 sc in next st, sc in each of next 2 sts, 2 sc in next st, sc in each of next 9 sts.

Round 3: Sc in each st around.

Round 4: Sc in each of next 8 sts, sc2tog, sc in each of next 7 sts, sc2tog, sc in each of next 8 sts.

Round 5: Sc in each of next 7 sts, sc2tog, sc in each of next 7 sts, sc2tog, sc in each of next 7 sts.

Round 6: Sc in each of next 8 sts, sc2tog, sc in each of next 5 sts, sc2tog, sc in each of next 6 sts.

Round 7: Sc in each of next 8 sts, sc2tog, sc in each of next 3 sts, sc2tog, sc in each of next 6 sts.

Round 8: Sc in each of next 10 sts, sc2tog, sc in each of next 7 sts.

Rounds 9–11: Sc in each st around.

Making the Front Legs

Step 1: Thread tapestry needle with new strand of gray yarn. Draw yarn through center stitch on opposite sides of body so there are 8 sts on each side for legs.

Step 2: Remove needle and tie a double knot in center as shown. Shove both yarn ends from knot tied into body.

Step 3: You should now have two separate openings for legs. Re-insert hook from where you stopped stitching at end of body and continue crocheting legs with yarn still attached.

For each leg: Rounds 1–3: Sc in each st around.

Step 4: After 3rd round of sc, fasten off, leaving long tail. Stuff with polyfill. Thread tapestry needle with yarn tail. Insert needle under front loop only of each sc around.

Step 5: Pull yarn tail to completely cinch leg closed as shown. Bring needle out elsewhere on body. Trim excess yarn.

Step 6: Attach new yarn at 2nd leg opening with a sl st and repeat rounds 1–3. After 3rd round of sc, repeat steps 4–5 to finish 2nd leg the same way.

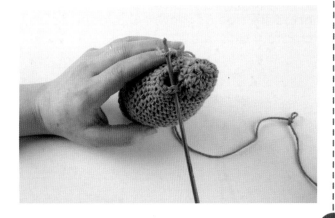

Assembly

With a tapestry needle and yarn tails, assemble cat as follows. Pin each part in desired position before sewing.

1. Sew ears onto either side of head.
2. Sew muzzle onto head under eyes, stuffing lightly with polyfill.
3. Add whiskers (see below).
4. Sew head onto body.
5. Sew tail onto body.
6. Make sure all ends are woven in.

Adding the Whiskers

Step 1: Thread tapestry needle with strand of black scrap yarn.

Step 2: Insert needle through one side of muzzle and out the opposite side as shown. Don't draw yarn all the way through; leave desired length of whiskers hanging.

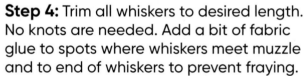

Step 4: Trim all whiskers to desired length. No knots are needed. Add a bit of fabric glue to spots where whiskers meet muzzle and to end of whiskers to prevent fraying.

Step 3: Insert needle through same side of muzzle you just exited from and out the opposite side as shown. Cut looped side to create 4 whiskers.